The Discovery Books are prepared
under the educational supervision of

Mary C. Austin, Ed.D.
Reading Specialist and
Professor of Education
Case Western Reserve University

A DISCOVERY BOOK

N

S

GARRARD PUBLISHING COMPANY
CHAMPAIGN, ILLINOIS

Lucretia Mott

Foe of Slavery

by Doris Faber

illustrated by Russell Hoover

Standard Book Number: 8116-6303-X
Library of Congress Catalog Card Number: 70–151992

Contents

Lucretia Mott: Foe of Slavery

Chapter 1

"A Ship! A Ship!"

"Lu, you do it!" Sarah said.

"Please, Lu," Eliza begged. "You had the idea in the first place."

Seven-year-old Lucretia Coffin looked fondly at her two sisters. Sarah was two years older; Eliza was almost two years younger. But they both thought she—Lucretia—should give their father the farewell present they had all made for him.

So Lucretia stepped forward on the dock

where last-minute preparations were being hurried. As soon as the tide changed, Captain Thomas Coffin's ship was going to sail. It was the spring of 1800. He was one of the brave New Englanders who had begun trading with far-off China.

"Can you stop a minute?" Lucretia asked, gently pulling at her father's arm. "We have something for you. It's to remind you we'll be counting the days till you return."

Captain Coffin was a tall, strong man whose face was tanned by the sun and wind. Now suddenly he seemed about to weep as he bent down and hugged his middle daughter.

Lucretia felt tears filling her own eyes. Still, she tried to smile. She handed him the bit of sewing the girls had worked on together. With neat stitches they had made a simple sort of calendar for two years. It would probably be that long before they saw him again.

"Thank you, my dear," Captain Coffin said warmly. "Thank you, Sarah and Eliza. Now here's your mother with your brother. Let me kiss each of you. Then I must go aboard."

Before long the ship had sailed, and the excitement of waving good-bye was over. Lucretia tried hard to hide her sadness. With her mother and sisters and little Tom, who was just three years old, she walked up the cobbled streets of Nantucket. Soon they reached their home. It was a white-frame cottage with a neat garden around it.

Nantucket is a small island about 30 miles off the mainland of Massachusetts. Lucretia had been born there on January 3, 1793. Her whole family, back to her great-grandfather, had lived on Nantucket. Many of the island's men were sailors on whaling ships or trading ships.

So the women and children of Nantucket learned to take care of themselves. After Captain Coffin left for China, Lucretia's mother started a small shop in their front parlor. Now she could earn some money while her husband was gone.

One summer morning Mrs. Coffin was busy in her shop. Sarah and Eliza were cleaning the house. Lucretia took Tom to gather beach plums. On their return, she began cooking a pot of jam.

"Lu, sing me a song," Tom begged.

Lucretia put down her spoon and drew in a deep breath. She sang: "Sing, sing, what shall I sing? The cat's run away with the pudding-bag string!"

Their mother opened the door from her shop. "Oh, Lucretia!" she said. "If you

were as far out of town as you are out of tune, you wouldn't get home tonight."

Lucretia laughed, then her sweet face became thoughtful. "Mama, would you rather I stopped trying to sing?" she asked. There was a good reason for the question.

The Coffins and their neighbors were all members of the same religious group. They were Quakers. At that time the Quaker faith was more strict than other religions. Their praying was direct and simple, and they tried to live as simply as possible. They wore plain gray or brown clothing everyday. Some Quakers did not even approve of music.

Still Lucretia saw no harm in singing. She thought that she should be able to decide about a matter like this.

Mrs. Coffin seemed to sense this. "Child," she said, "sing if you wish."

Lucretia broke into a smile again. From then on, she hummed softly as she sat knitting socks for Tom. She sang while she walked to school with Sarah and Eliza. When spring came again, she made her sisters laugh by imitating the songs of the birds sitting on the chimney.

Lucretia did not know that some people thought Quakers never enjoyed themselves. She had a cheerful nature, and she was part of a happy family. She loved Nantucket—its cobbled streets, its busy waterfront, and its windswept beaches. However, she did have a secret worry.

Suppose her father's ship met trouble? Month after month passed, and she prayed for him nightly. When two years had gone by without any word, Lucretia still did not speak of her fears. Instead, she did all she could to cheer her mother and her sisters. "Should I recite the entire multiplication table *backwards*?" she would ask if someone looked sad.

Even Lucretia lost heart, though, when three whole years had passed and her father had not returned. Then on a fine spring morning, the cry arose: "A ship! A ship!"

This time Lucretia was not disappointed. Only a few hours later Captain Coffin walked down the gangplank and rushed to throw his arms around his waiting family.

Chapter 2

Boston

"I have news for you," Captain Coffin said at the dinner table a few weeks later.

Lucretia put down her spoon. What was her father planning? He had just come back from a short trip to Boston. Would he be sailing soon on a ship from that city?

"No, I will not leave you again," Captain Coffin told his family with a smile. "I have had enough of the sea.

Now I hope to be a merchant. As soon as I can make the necessary arrangements, we are moving to Boston."

Lucretia clapped a hand to her mouth. Visiting Boston was the most wonderful thing she could think of. However, living there meant no more happy days on Nantucket. How could she give up the only home she had ever known?

These thoughts kept returning to Lucretia during the next few months. While her father looked after business matters, she and her sisters helped their mother pack. Then as moving day drew closer, the girls could not hold back their tears.

Still, Lucretia's first sight of Boston almost made up for all the sadness. As she stepped off the bobbing little ship, she stared in amazement at streets filled with carts and wagons. More people than she had ever imagined crowded the sidewalks.

Many things in Boston surprised Lucretia. The greatest surprise was a red-brick schoolhouse around the corner from the Coffins' new home. Both boys and girls were taught there. On Nantucket a lady had given lessons to a few pupils in her front parlor.

For more than a year, Lucretia went to this new school with her sisters. Then she began to feel restless. She did not like to trouble her parents, but she thought she had learned all she could there. Happily, her father felt the same way.

"Lucretia," he said one evening after he had listened to her recite a long poem by heart, "I believe you have a keen mind. I think you should be given the chance for more education."

"I would like that," she said quickly.

"Unfortunately, only a few schools offer advanced work to girls," he went on. "None of these is in Boston. However, I have written to find out about a school some Quakers have started in New York State. Would you be willing to leave your family to go there?"

Lucretia gasped. She was not sure. However, she was nearly thirteen. The idea of stepping out into the world pleased her.

"I—I would like to go there," she said.

Chapter 3

Nine Partners

"Step carefully," Captain Coffin warned.

Lucretia held her long gray skirt a little above her ankles and climbed into the coach. She and her father were starting on the long ride to New York State. The trip would take at least 30 hours, without counting stops where the horses would be changed.

How that coach bounced! Lucretia slept part of the time. Still, she was very tired when they finally arrived at the school.

It was a large, square building set in a park.

"I—I am sure I'm going to like it here," Lucretia said bravely. Yet she already felt lonesome.

Her first weeks at boarding school were the worst she had ever known. After her father left, she missed her dear family every minute of the day. Often at night, her pillow was wet with tears.

Yet, sitting in her classes, she looked calm. No one could have guessed how homesick she was. Although slim and not very tall, she looked older than she really was.

Gradually Lucretia started to feel at home at the Nine Partners School. Its odd name came from the fact that nine men had once owned this land in the Hudson River's green valley. Lucretia liked the school much more after she made friends with the golden-haired girl who sat next to her in English class.

"You don't seem lonely," the girl said. "Yet I think you must be. All new girls are. Won't you be friends with me? My name is Sarah Mott."

Lucretia smiled. "I have a sister named Sarah at home," she said. The thought of home almost made her burst into tears.

"Let me be your sister while you're here," Sarah Mott whispered as the teacher entered the room.

Before long Lucretia and Sarah did become almost as close as sisters. Because travel to Boston was so difficult, Lucretia spent school vacations visiting Sarah's family in New York State. When she was thirteen, she met Sarah's brother James, who was eighteen. A year later James became a teacher in the boys' school.

Boys were taught in one part of the

Nine Partners School, and girls in another. They were not supposed to play with one another. However, Lucretia once crossed over to the boys' side to help a boy who was being punished by being kept in his room without food. She smuggled bread and milk to him.

Sometimes Lucretia managed to talk to Sarah's brother James over the fence which separated the boys' and girls' playgrounds. Although James seemed rather shy, Lucretia enjoyed asking him questions. Soon he felt at ease with her.

"Is it fair that school fees are the same for boys and girls, although boys are taught more subjects? Why can't girls study the same things as boys?" Lucretia asked James these questions, and he thought about them.

"Yes," he decided, "girls should be allowed to study the same subjects."

"Is it not possible for a girl to become a good teacher?" she asked.

James thought about this too. Then he said that a girl might surely turn into a fine teacher.

At sixteen, Lucretia herself was offered the job of assistant teacher in the girls' school. Her first thought, even before writing home to her parents, was to ask James what he thought about the offer.

"I would be pleased if you became a teacher here," he said in his most serious tone. There was a smile about his eyes, though, that Lucretia could not understand.

A few months later, when the term was almost ended, Lucretia asked him another important question.

"Do you think it is right," she said, "that I am not being paid for my work? Even the head of the girls' school earns only $20 a term. Yet you and the other men teachers are paid much more."

They were walking in the garden, and nobody else was in sight. James suddenly reached down and took Lucretia's hand.

"No, I think that is wrong," he said. "But I beg you not to worry about it now. You ought not to plan to be a teacher much longer. I would like you to become my wife."

Lucretia was so surprised that, for once, she could not say a word. Still, she nodded her head in happy agreement with this wonderful idea.

Chapter 4

A New Name

"I, Lucretia, take thee, James Mott, to be my husband," the eighteen-year-old bride said happily. It was April 10, 1811, Lucretia and James' wedding day, in the Pine Street Meeting House in Philadelphia.

Captain Coffin had moved his family to this city to make a fresh start in business. When the captain's new nail factory and store in Philadelphia began to do well, he sent for James Mott to help him. Soon after, Lucretia and James were married.

The former sea captain was happy to have James Mott for a son-in-law. He also thought James had a good head for business, so he asked him to be his partner. The new sign hanging over his warehouse near Philadelphia's waterfront read "Coffin and Mott—Merchants."

While James and her father worked together, the new Mrs. Mott happily began housekeeping. She and James lived in a few small rooms in a narrow old brick building. It was around the corner from the larger house where the rest of Lucretia's family lived.

"I cannot tell you how pleased I am to be close to you again," she kept telling her mother and sisters.

The year after her marriage, young Mrs. Mott gave birth to a daughter.

The baby was named Anna after Mrs. Coffin. Two years later Lucretia had a son, Thomas, named for his grandfather.

Mrs. Mott loved playing games with her children. She taught them to read as soon as they were old enough. She also taught other children in a school for girls which she and a cousin ran for a time.

When her sisters married she helped them get settled in their new homes. These were happy years for her. Then suddenly her father became ill with typhus fever and died. Mrs. Mott did all she could to comfort her mother.

A few years later another fever struck Mrs. Mott's own household. Her three-year-old son became ill, and no medicine seemed to help him. Within a week he died.

Mrs. Mott felt so sad about his death

that she herself became ill. When she finally did get well again, she was a more serious person. She turned to religion and spent long hours alone reading her Bible. Then she came to a surprising decision.

"Lucretia has taken up the preaching line," her mother wrote to relatives.

Although there were no women ministers in other religious groups, the Quakers did have some. Any member who felt the call could become a minister, if a committee of elders approved. When Lucretia Mott was 28, she became a minister and spoke at several of the Quaker meeting houses in and around Philadelphia.

Mrs. Mott also kept a lively interest in the world around her. When a man named Benjamin Lundy called a meeting to talk about slavery, she went to hear him speak. This was a great turning point in her life.

Lundy had just come back from a visit to Virginia. There he had been shocked by the sight of a slave market. He had heard the terrible cries of black children who were taken from their parents. He decided to spend the rest of his life doing all he could to end slavery.

Lucretia Mott was deeply moved by Lundy's words. Like many other Quakers, she had already come to feel that slavery was wrong. Now she spoke to her husband, who had become a cotton merchant after Captain Coffin's death.

"James," she said, "I do not think you should continue to sell cotton goods. They have been made with the labor of slaves. I would rather go hungry than earn money from the suffering of others."

James Mott listened to her thoughtfully. He agreed with Lucretia, but he worried about earning enough money to support his family. Finally he decided to do as Lucretia suggested.

As a result, Mr. Mott soon left the cotton trade. He began to sell only woolen goods in his new store on Front Street. Still Mrs. Mott did not think she had done enough. She got a group of wives together. "We must promise each other to stop buying things made by the labor of slaves," she said.

Chapter 5

Speaking Up

As time went by, Mrs. Mott had four more babies. Three of them were girls named Maria, Elizabeth, and Martha. She also had a son named Thomas in memory of the boy who had died.

"I'm busy as a beaver," she wrote to one of her married sisters. "Before breakfast, I do my dusting and sweeping. While the children nap, I make bread and apple pies. After dinner, I try to catch up with my reading."

She also spoke every week at Quaker meetings. When her children grew older and needed her less, she spent more and more of her time working against slavery.

The Motts now had a large house with a comfortable parlor. Here Mrs. Mott welcomed company almost every evening.

"The millions of slaves in our land are the most badly treated group in this country," she would say in her clear, sweet voice. "I feel bound to do all in my power to win freedom for them."

Then she would tell her visitors about the new antislavery society she was helping to plan. Its members were going to hold public meetings against slavery. They would also publish books and newspapers. Their aim would be to convince as many people as possible that slavery ought to be outlawed.

"Similar groups are being formed in

other cities in the North," Mrs. Mott would add. "Indeed, a man from Boston is hoping to unite them all into one group."

His name was William Lloyd Garrison. Unlike Mrs. Mott and her husband, who was quietly encouraging her, Garrison liked the idea of upsetting people.

"I WILL BE HEARD!" he shouted. He forced people to pay attention to a problem they had been trying to ignore. Most Northerners still thought that Southern people should decide for themselves whether or not there would be slaves. Garrison did not agree with this. Instead, he said that Northerners had to make Southerners understand that slavery was wrong.

Mrs. Mott felt just the way he did. However, she never shouted at people who did not agree with her. Instead she tried to reason with them. She even read them a simple little verse:

If slavery comes by color,
which God gave,
Fashion may change,
and you become the slave.

Still, she helped Mr. Garrison in many ways. In 1833 he decided to call a national meeting of antislavery societies. It was to be held in Philadelphia. She told him to use her house as his home away from home. She also did something far more daring.

Mrs. Mott took a seat at the back of the hall on the day the meeting started. With her were a few dozen other women, most of them Quakers. Like her, they had been working to make this gathering a success. However, it was well understood

that they must sit quietly. Only the men would talk at the meeting.

Yet Mrs. Mott found that she could not stay silent. When a few men began to argue about what the group's aims should be, she stood up.

"I respectfully suggest," she said, "that we leave out the last two lines in Mr. Garrison's statement. Then it should satisfy all who are objecting."

A buzz of surprised voices arose as she took her seat again. None of those present had ever heard a woman speak at a public gathering. Some men thought that women should remain silent at home when important matters were discussed, and leave all decisions to men.

Still, what Mrs. Mott said made very good sense, and she spoke politely. The chairman rapped for order and then praised her.

Chapter 6

“On to Motts’!”

Soon after the convention ended, Mrs. Mott helped to form the Philadelphia Female Anti-Slavery Society.

“In our own city, we women can do something that very much needs to be done,” Mrs. Mott said.

So she and several Quaker friends visited the small group of black families living in Philadelphia. These families had won their freedom from slavery. However, they faced problems of every kind. The men had trouble finding jobs. Few schools welcomed their children.

Even so, they had not lost hope, for there were Negroes like James Forten and his wife who helped them. Mr. Forten was a fine sailmaker and a natural leader. He owned his own business and served as the unofficial mayor of the black people of Philadelphia.

"We thank you for offering to help us," he told Mrs. Mott. "We like your plan of giving reading lessons to our boys and girls. But we would like to help too. Nobody can feel more deeply than we do about the need to free black people in the South. Will you let my wife join in your work?"

"That would please me very much," Mrs. Mott said.

For the next few years, the Female Anti-Slavery Society quietly did some useful work. A small school was started for black children. Black women were given sewing

lessons. Food and medicine were provided for needy families.

Black women and white women worked together on these projects. Still, many Northerners did not agree with the antislavery movement. They thought that abolitionists, as antislavery people were called, were just stirring up trouble. "Black people are not the same as we are," they said. "They should not be treated as equals." Many felt that whites and blacks should not attend the same meetings.

In Philadelphia, in 1838, these feelings became stronger than ever.

A fine new meeting hall had just been built in the main part of the city. Several religious groups had given money to make this a center for antislavery programs. Mrs. Mott had invited women from antislavery societies in other cities to attend a meeting in Philadelphia. She hoped they would be able to plan new ways to work to end slavery.

However, on the day the meeting opened a crowd of hoodlums gathered near the door of the hall. They shouted nasty words when white women and black women walked in together.

Mrs. Mott calmly rose to begin the meeting. "I hope," she said, "that no person will be alarmed by a little *appearance* of danger."

Yet the danger was real. That evening, after the women had left, a mob angrily set the new meeting hall on fire.

The hall was empty then, so no lives were lost. But the sight of the fine building going up in flames was not enough to satisfy the howling crowd. Someone remembered that Lucretia Mott was the leader of the women's group.

"On to Motts'!" The mob took up this terrible cry.

Meanwhile, half a mile away a few dozen men and women were sitting in the Motts' parlor talking about the meeting. Then came a loud knock at the front door. A breathless young man entered. He had never forgotten that Mrs. Mott had brought food and money to his family while his father was out of work. He quickly told her what was happening.

Mrs. Mott looked across the room at her husband. These two knew each other so well that they needed no words. James Mott rose and went upstairs to get their young children. Then he took them to a neighbor's house for safety. A few minutes later he returned and calmly sat down again next to his wife. They were ready to face whatever might come.

However, the young man who had warned them was now hurrying back toward the center of town. When he met the mob he grabbed the elbow of one of the leaders. "The Motts' home is this way!" he cried. Purposely he pointed in the wrong direction.

The trick worked.

When the hoodlums could not find the Motts' house, they began to drift away. Mr. and Mrs. Mott were safe. After the danger had passed, Mrs. Mott spoke quietly to her husband. "I felt willing to suffer whatever the cause required," she said.

Chapter 7

With Lizzie in London

Why had no police been sent to control the mob?

Many fair-minded people asked this question when they read about what had happened. The mayor of Philadelphia saw to it that antislavery meetings were well protected from then on.

During the next two years, Mrs. Mott spent more and more time giving speeches about slavery. She spoke to Quakers, and she spoke to many other religious groups.

"We all try to teach our children the difference between right and wrong," she told them. "Let us remember this difference ourselves. We must never forget that slavery is *wrong*!

"Slavery cannot be ended here," she went on, "until the majority of people in America realize it is evil."

Mrs. Mott's hard work brought her an unexpected reward. In 1840 Garrison's American Anti-Slavery Society asked her to go to England. An antislavery meeting of people from all over the world was being planned in London. Four other American women were elected to attend the meeting too.

Mrs. Mott was now 47. However, she felt as excited as a girl at the idea of making this trip. Her children were all old enough so she could safely leave them with relatives for a few months.

Her husband was going with her. He would be a delegate too.

"We sail from New York on the fifth of May," Mrs. Mott wrote happily to one of her sisters. "I do so look forward to it."

Soon after arriving in London, Mrs. Mott made a disturbing discovery. Although the American women had come a great distance, they were unwelcome. "This convention is not for women," Lucretia was told by an English abolitionist. "Women are unfit to attend meetings with men."

"It is surprising that *you* should think so," she told the abolitionist. "Those are the same words slave owners use when saying black people are unfit to be with whites."

"We hope you will not insist on being seated at the meeting," said another man.

Lucretia and the other American ladies had talked this over. "We were elected by our antislavery societies to represent them," Lucretia told the Englishman politely. "We feel it is our duty to attend."

When the convention opened, James Mott and the other men took their places on the hall floor. Lucretia and the ladies were led to a balcony and seated behind a curtain. They were hidden from the view of the men delegates.

Lucretia shook her head. "This is too bad," she said.

"It surely is!" a dark-haired young woman cried.

She was the wife of a New York abolitionist who was attending the meeting. She had married him only a few weeks earlier and this trip was her honeymoon. As Miss Lizzie Cady, she had resented not only slavery, but also the unfair way women were treated. Her father was a judge, and she liked to read his law books. "Why can't girls become lawyers?" she kept asking him. "Why can't we go to college? What sense does it make to keep girls from using the brains God gave them?"

Now, as Mrs. Elizabeth Cady Stanton, she decided something had to be done.

"It's time," Lizzie Stanton sputtered to Mrs. Mott. "It's time some demand is made for new rights for women."

Mrs. Mott thought back to her own experiences as a teacher. She had been paid not a penny for her work, while men teachers earned fair salaries. She thought it most unjust for women to be kept from speaking at this abolitionist meeting.

"I agree with you, my dear," she said. "Let's discuss it after the meeting."

Chapter 8

Busy Years

Before they left London, Mrs. Mott and Mrs. Stanton made a promise to each other. They would work on woman's rights as soon as possible. However, one thing after another kept them from doing this —including the "underground railroad."

Ever since the early 1800s, some of Philadelphia's Quakers had been doing all they could to help runaway slaves. James and Lucretia Mott were proud to have their house serve as a station for these travelers from the South. Shortly after the Motts returned from Europe, they had an exciting few weeks.

First, they received word that a slave named Henry Brown had made up his mind to escape from the South. He had himself nailed in a box addressed to the Anti-Slavery Society in Philadelphia. It was loaded aboard a train in Virginia.

When that train finally arrived in the Philadelphia depot, James Mott and other members of the society were waiting. Workmen quickly lifted the box onto a wagon.

The men drove then to the office of the Anti-Slavery Society and carried the box safely indoors. One of them tapped gently on the wooden top.

"Are you all right?" he asked.

From inside the box a faint tap sounded. "All right, sir," a muffled voice said.

Until he got back his strength, Henry "Box" Brown stayed hidden in an upstairs room at the Motts'. Then James and Lucretia gave him food and money and directions to his next stop. Brown left Philadelphia on his way to freedom in Canada.

Soon after this Mrs. Mott went on a speaking trip. It took her through many northern states, then into slave states. In churches and in meeting halls, she spoke without fear against slavery. Once her coach was hit with stones. At another meeting a riot broke out.

A clergyman at this meeting took her arm to lead her to safety. But she asked him to help some other women through the angry crowd.

"Who will take care of you?" the worried minister asked her.

"This man!" she said, putting her hand on the arm of one of the rioters. The man's mouth opened wide in surprise, but he did lead her through the mob. When some of his friends began teasing him, he said, "Well, she's a good, sensible woman. You can see that."

Wherever she spoke, people were impressed by Mrs. Mott. Many expected a woman speaker to be strange and unladylike. They were always surprised when they first saw her. In her Quaker bonnet and gray gown, she was the picture of a gentle woman. The tone of her voice was soft, and she never argued with her listeners. She tried to reason with them the way a good teacher would.

Mrs. Mott became so famous that she was invited to tea at the White House. There she tried to make President Tyler believe in the rightness of her cause.

"If all of your friends were as reasonable as you are, ma'am, I'd have more hope of solving this problem," he told her. The Virginia-born president was himself a slave owner.

Month after month, Mrs. Mott kept speaking at antislavery meetings in many cities. Year after year, she traveled wherever she thought she might do some good. Even those who did not agree with her about slavery gradually came to admire her.

In between meetings Mrs. Mott was busy with her family. In the summer of 1848 she visited a married sister who had moved to New York State. Her sister's home was near the village of Seneca Falls, where Elizabeth Cady Stanton now lived. So it happened that these two women finally met again.

Chapter 9

The Right Time

"We must not wait any longer!" Lizzie Stanton said.

Mrs. Mott smiled. Her young friend had not grown more patient since becoming the mother of several lively little boys. The moment Lizzie heard Lucretia Mott had arrived in the area, she left her boys with a neighbor and drove over to see her. Lizzie was demanding that they keep their promise to each other about working for woman's rights. They must hold a meeting at once.

"What good would it do to have a

meeting in this country village?" Mrs. Mott asked gently.

"Some other ideas that have traveled far were thought of first right here!" Mrs. Stanton said.

Mrs. Mott had to admit this was true. "But is it a good plan to hold a meeting during the summer?" she asked. "Won't the wives of farmers be too busy to come?"

"We have waited too long already!"

Without another word Mrs. Stanton

reached for a pen and paper. Then she wrote:

> WOMAN'S RIGHTS CONVENTION—A Convention to discuss the social, civil, and religious condition and rights of women, will be held in the Wesleyan Chapel, at Seneca Falls, N.Y., on Wednesday and Thursday, the 19th and 20th of July, current, starting at 10 o'clock, A.M. The public generally are invited to be present. . . . Lucretia Mott of Philadelphia . . . will address the Convention.

This was printed in the next issue of the local newspaper. Mrs. Mott was too modest to think that mention of her name would draw people from miles around. But nearly 300 women—and a good many men

—did come to Seneca Falls.

Speaking with deep feeling, Mrs. Mott told them that the time had come for starting a movement for woman's rights. One of its main aims, she and Mrs. Stanton had decided, was to gain equal educational opportunities for girls. Schools should teach girls the same subjects as boys, and colleges should open their doors to women. Women should have the right to work at other jobs besides just sewing and teaching. They should be able to be doctors, lawyers, and business leaders. They ought to be paid for their work at the same rate as men.

After almost every sentence a burst of clapping made Mrs. Mott wait for silence. When at last she finished, she called on Mrs. Elizabeth Cady Stanton.

Mrs. Stanton rose. She began to read sentences that had a familiar ring.

"We hold these truths to be self-evident," she read, "that all men *and women* are created equal."

The audience gasped at this bold change in the words of the Declaration of Independence. But that was only the beginning of Mrs. Stanton's boldness. She then read the rest of her own version of the famous words Thomas Jefferson had written in 1776.

Jefferson had listed the wrongs that led the thirteen colonies to break away from England. Mrs. Stanton gave one example after another of the wrongs suffered by the women of the United States. She pointed out that married women could not own property. If they did earn money, every penny belonged by law to their husbands.

Many changes had to come, she said. Unfair laws had to be changed. Schools and businesses must begin to treat men and women equally. Most important of all, the women of America must be given the right to vote.

"Why, Lizzie," Mrs. Mott broke in gently, "you will make us laughed at!"

To most people in 1848, giving women the right to vote was a daring idea. Mrs. Mott knew that many people would object. She feared the whole woman's rights program would become a joke.

"No!" said Lizzie Stanton. "Without the vote we will still be second-class citizens, even if we can go to college and earn equal money."

Mrs. Mott thought about this. "Perhaps you are right," she said finally.

After two days of talk, the people at the meeting agreed to work for woman's rights. A great new movement was on its way!

Chapter 10

Progress?

"You were certainly right, Lucretia," Lizzie Stanton said cheerfully. She held up a newspaper that had just arrived by mail from Massachusetts.

On its front page was a story Mrs. Mott read with a sad little smile. If only men would take the women's plans seriously! Like dozens of other editors, this one was treating the woman's rights meeting in Seneca Falls as a great joke.

PROGRESS? was the headline.

Then the story went on to poke fun at the idea of women wanting to change places with men. Wouldn't it be wonderful, the writer asked, if men took up washing dishes and mending clothes while their wives ran the country?

However, many women did not agree with the editors. After returning to Philadelphia, Mrs. Mott received dozens of letters. "Thank you for calling attention to our problems," she was told again and again.

It took Lizzie Stanton, though, to think of another idea. This one really made people talk about the woman's rights movement.

Mrs. Stanton had a cousin who had spent some time visiting Turkey. This cousin had brought back some trousers worn by women in that country. Lizzie at once decided this costume was much more practical than the long skirts American women wore.

So she sewed herself a pair of floppy trousers something like the Turkish ones, topped by a short skirt. Unfortunately, these did not fit her very well. Still, she wore them everywhere. She cheerfully ignored the teasing that followed. "It's such a relief not to have a skirt trailing in the mud," she wrote to Mrs. Mott.

However, Mrs. Stanton was not satisfied yet. She had a friend in Seneca Falls, a widow named Mrs. Amelia Bloomer, who published a ladies' magazine. Mrs. Stanton asked her to print a picture of the Turkish trousers. Then supporters of woman's rights all over the United States could make them and enjoy freedom from long skirts. Soon these trousers came to be called "bloomers."

Within a few months, the whole country was laughing at women wearing bloomers.

Bands of little boys chanted:

Hi! Ho! In rain and snow,
The bloomer now is all the go!

Lucretia Mott never wore bloomers herself. She was too set in her ways to try a new style of dress. But she believed others should do as they wished.

Still she did tell her true feelings to her husband. "I hardly blame people for laughing," she said. "Those pantaloons do look very funny."

She was happy when Mrs. Stanton finally gave up wearing bloomers. She was also pleased when a young schoolteacher named Susan B. Anthony began to work for the cause of woman's rights.

Mrs. Mott knew that she herself was no longer able to do all she wanted to. Before breakfast every morning she still shelled peas or did other household jobs. She had company for dinner almost everyday. But as her sixtieth birthday neared, she finally began obeying her family's wishes to cut down on her work.

She could not refuse to go to the most important woman's rights meetings, of course. She still spoke at these gatherings. Her speeches were treated with respect by newspapers that otherwise poked fun at "hen conventions." Yet now she was glad to leave the hard work of planning new programs in Susan Anthony's strong hands.

In antislavery work, her speeches were no longer as necessary as in the past. Public opinion had changed. "Now," Lucretia told her husband, "most people in the North agree that slavery is wrong." Lucretia knew that the antislavery work was being carried on by able men in politics. They were working to pass laws to stop slavery. Still, a terrible question remained.

How were the slaves to be freed without a war between the North and the South?

As a Quaker Mrs. Mott had always hated fighting. "I am for peace," she said again and again. Word came one day that shooting had started in South Carolina. The nation was torn by a civil war. Mrs. Mott shut herself up in her room to pray.

She liked President Lincoln, but she could not speak in favor of the war.

By this time the Motts were living in the country outside Philadelphia. In 1857 James had decided that the time had come for him to retire from his business. So he bought a farm called Roadside, where tall trees shaded the front lawn. Here his wife enjoyed picking strawberries and making jam as she had done so long ago on Nantucket.

Here too she enjoyed one of the happiest days of her life. On a bright spring morning friends and relatives came to the farm. It was the fiftieth wedding anniversary of James and Lucretia Mott.

Their married daughters and their son all came with their own families. With her grandchildren around her, Mrs. Mott sat holding one tiny great-grandchild on her lap.

She had always wanted very little for herself. So there was a problem about choosing a gift to give her on her golden wedding anniversary. But her dear ones solved it neatly—by presenting her with a pair of gold knitting needles.

"I shall remember this beautiful day whenever I use them," she said with tears of happiness in her eyes.

Another great day came in 1862 when the president signed the Emancipation Proclamation. Lucretia went to a joyful meeting of the Female Anti-Slavery Society. Their long years of work had not been wasted. The Southern slaves were free!

Soon Negro soldiers, among the first blacks allowed in the army, were training at a camp near Roadside. Mrs. Mott took the men baskets of fruit, and homemade cakes and pies.

The war was still far from over. Even when she worked in her quiet garden, Mrs. Mott could not forget it. She worried about her nephews and the sons of friends who were in the midst of the fighting. And she grieved, because she still felt war was wrong.

Chapter 11

"Yes, I Must Rest"

Mrs. Mott was joyful when the Civil War ended. She was pleased that Negro men now had the right to vote. But she was disappointed that women had not been given the same right to vote. In letters to Lizzie Stanton and Susan Anthony, she made no secret of her feelings.

"I am much pleased to hear that there are many young people who are willing to give time and talent to the woman's cause," she wrote. "Give me *noise* on this subject!"

Yet she herself felt a growing need for peace and quiet. Those in the fight for woman's rights, however, still thought of her as their leader. They often came to ask her advice. After one such visit she wrote in her diary:

"This equal rights movement is no play —but I cannot enter into it. Just hearing their talk made me ache all over, and be glad to come away and lie on the sofa. Yes, I must rest."

Mrs. Mott grew even weaker when she had to bear a great loss. Her beloved husband caught a cold five months before his eightieth birthday. He became seriously ill a few days later. Within the week, he died.

Lucretia Mott was then 74. It took her many months to get over her sorrow. Still, she surprised everyone by once again taking a lively interest in the world.

She even went on several trips by train to see her children and grandchildren. And she still showed the same independence that she always had had. When relatives wanted to take her home, she would say, "No, thank you, I don't need anyone. There is always somebody to help me in and out of the cars."

Mrs. Mott attended a public meeting from time to time. When she was 85 she went to the thirtieth anniversary of the Seneca Falls meeting.

Frail as she was, she walked alone into the meeting hall. Frederick Douglass, the former slave who had become a great leader of the black citizens of America, was on the platform. He was speaking about the importance of getting equal rights for all citizens—black and white, male and female. He stopped speaking and walked forward to welcome Mrs. Mott.

Applause seemed to shake the very walls as he led her up onto the platform. With the gentle smile those present knew so well, Mrs. Mott tried to make herself heard above the cheering. "Thank you," she said. "Thank you all."

After she finished speaking, and with the same smile, she started walking alone down the steps toward the door. Speaking for that whole audience, Frederick Douglass called, "Good-bye, Lucretia!"

Back at home on her farm outside Philadelphia, cared for by loving friends, Mrs. Mott lived for two more years. She died in her sleep on November 11, 1880.

In many parts of the United States, solemn meetings were held. Quakers and people of other faiths wanted to pay their last respects to Lucretia Mott. "She was a rare person," many said. "She was never afraid to speak up against injustice."